21st Century Skills Library

LIFE SKILLS BIOGRAPHIES

MAGIC JOHNSON

Ellen Labrecque

Cherry Lake Publishing
Ann Arbor, Michigan

Published in the United States of America by Cherry Lake Publishing
Ann Arbor, MI
www.cherrylakepublishing.com

Content Adviser: Matt Zeysing, Historian and Archivist, Naismith Memorial Basketball
Hall of Fame, Springfield, Massachusetts

Photo Credits: Cover, © Neal Preston/CORBIS; pages 6, 10, 13, 14, 16, 18, 20, 23, 24,
27, © Bettmann/CORBIS; page 29, © Steven Georges/Press-Telegram/Corbis; page 30,
© Hashimoto Noboru/CORBIS SYGMA; page 32, © SOQUI TED/CORBIS SYGMA;
page 34, © Gregg Newton/CORBIS; page 37, Neal Preston/CORBIS; page 38, © Reuters/
CORBIS; page 39, © Chris Pizzello/CNN/Handout/Reuters/Corbis; page 40, © Steve
Marcus/Las Vegas Sun/Reuters/Corbis; page 42, © Lori Conn/ZUMA/Corbis

Library of Congress Cataloging-in-Publication Data
Labrecque, Ellen.
  Magic Johnson / by Ellen Labrecque.
    p. cm.—(Life skills biographies)
  ISBN-13: 978-1-60279-071-1
  ISBN-10: 1-60279-071-X
  1. Johnson, Earvin, 1959—Juvenile literature. 2. Basketball players—United States—
Biography—Juvenile literature. I. Title. II. Series.
  GV884.J64L33 2008
  796.323092—dc22
  [B]   2007008646

Cherry Lake Publishing would like to acknowledge the work of
The Partnership for 21st Century Skills.
Please visit www.21stcenturyskills.org for more information.

CONTENTS

INTRODUCTION

Game 6 of the 1980 National Basketball Association (NBA) Championship between the Los Angeles Lakers and the Philadelphia 76ers was about to begin. The Lakers led the best-of-seven-games series 3–2. But their star center, Kareem Abdul-Jabbar, was sidelined with a sprained ankle. One of his teammates was point guard Magic Johnson, age 20, a rookie who had left college to join the pros. Standing 6 feet 9 (2.1 meters), Magic was the tallest point guard in NBA history. But for Game 6, Magic would have to play center in place of Abdul-Jabbar, or his team would lose.

Magic not only played center, he played the best game of his career. He scored 42 points, grabbed 15 rebounds, made 7 assists, had 3 steals, and blocked 1 shot. The Lakers won the game 123–107 and the NBA championship 4–2.

"It was amazing, just amazing," Philadelphia's star Julius Erving told *Sports Illustrated* after the game. "Magic was outstanding. Unreal."

Magic is one of the greatest basketball players in history. He played 13 seasons in the NBA, all with the Los Angeles Lakers. He helped his team win 5 NBA championships. He also won the Most Valuable Player (MVP) award 3 times and the NBA championship MVP 3 times, and played on the All-Star team 12 times. Magic wasn't just a star as a professional; he also excelled at the high school and college levels. He was named a McDonald's All-American at Everett High School in Lansing, Michigan, and he was twice named All-America at Michigan State while leading the Spartans to the national title in 1979.

Off the court—as a businessman, philanthropist, and spokesperson—he's proved himself to be just as outstanding. His life journey has been nothing short of magical.

∾

CHAPTER ONE

THE EARLY YEARS

Earvin Johnson Jr. was born on August 14, 1959, in Lansing, Michigan. He was the fourth of seven children. His family did not have a lot of money, but there was always plenty of love to go around. The Johnsons

It was clear from an early age that Earvin Johnson Jr. (number 33) was going to be spectacular on the basketball court.

only had three bedrooms in their house: one for Earvin's mom and dad, one for the three boys, and one for the four girls. His father, Earvin Sr., worked nights at the General Motors automobile body plant and had a part-time job during the day. At one point, he worked as a janitor; at another time, he ran his own trash-collecting business. Earvin's mother, Christine, worked at a junior high school cafeteria.

Earvin's parents worked hard, and he soon followed their example. At age 10, he ran his own lawn-cutting business. At age 15, he was a stock boy at the local Dairy Queen. While Earvin toiled at these jobs, his mind was often elsewhere, dreaming about basketball. His boss at Dairy Queen remembers that Earvin always showed up to work with a basketball under his arm—Earvin would dribble all the way to work.

Earvin and his dad shared a love of basketball. On Sundays, father and son would sit on the couch and watch NBA games on television. "When the game was over," he said in his autobiography, *My Life*, "Dad would

The most important part of Earvin Johnson's life is his family. His parents have had a huge influence on him. He says he inherited his outgoing personality from his mom: "People talk about my smile, but my smile is [my mom's] smile. . . . Christine Johnson can make you happy by doing almost anything. She just lights up every place she goes."

And it was his dad who taught him to work hard and stay humble. In junior high, Earvin's basketball games were on Friday nights. Sometimes he would score 30 or 40 points. His dad was proud of him, but he didn't let Earvin get a big head. When his father ran a trash business, he roused his son from his bed at 6:30 A.M., even after a big game. Earvin still had to help out: "Maybe I was the hero of the game, but when I got home I still had to take out the trash."

sometimes come over with me to the Main Street courts near our house to practice some of the moves we had just seen."

When Earvin wasn't working, going to school, or watching basketball, he was on the court playing. If it was raining outside, he would roll up his dad's socks and shoot them into the laundry basket. If it snowed, he would shovel the playground and play full-court one-on-one with his brother Larry. He even woke up before dawn with basketball on his mind. If it was too early to go to the courts, he would dribble the ball on the street and pretend the parked cars were defenders. "All up and down the street people used to open their windows and yell at me for waking them up," he said. "But I couldn't help it. The game was just in me."

BECOMING MAGIC

In his sophomore year at Everett High School, he was chosen as a starter on the school's team. Earvin, who was 6 feet 5 (2 m) by his freshman year, didn't play just one position—he played them all. He jumped at center for the team, but he also brought the ball up the court as a point guard. Then he played near the basket as a forward. In other words, wherever Earvin played, he was unstoppable.

Earvin stood out for his outstanding play on the court and his outstanding attitude off the court. He hustled in practice, showed up early, and stayed late—always with a huge grin on his face. His white teeth and sparking eyes lit up any court, or room for that matter.

In one matchup his sophomore season, he had an exceptional game even by his standards. He scored 36 points, grabbed 18 rebounds, dished

14 assists, and made 5 steals. After the game, Fred Stabley Jr., a sportswriter for the local paper, the *Lansing State Journal,* came up to Earvin and said, "Listen, Earvin, I think you should have a nickname. I was thinking of calling you Dr. J., but that's taken. And so is Big E—Elvin Hayes. How about if I call you Magic?"

The name was perfect because Earvin's skills were magical. From that day on, Earvin Johnson Jr. was known as Magic.

Growing up with six brothers and sisters, Magic was taught to share, and he did so willingly. But when he was a senior on his high school team, he was a much better player than any of his teammates. It made sense to him to score himself instead of sharing the ball. He averaged a startling 45 points per game early in the season. Soon though his coach, George Fox, taught him an important lesson—that his performance was hurting the team, not helping them.

"You're scoring too much," Fox told him. "If we're going to win the championship this year, it'll take a team effort. The other guys have to get used to taking some important shots. You need to distribute the ball. Get those other guys involved more."

Magic took this lesson to heart. "I listened, and I changed my game," he said.

His scoring average dropped to just under 29 points per game as he passed the ball at every opportunity. But his team won the Michigan Class A State Championship. Throughout the rest of his career, Magic's ability to share the ball was the best and most important part of his game.

CHAPTER TWO

COLLEGE BOUND

*Hundreds of college coaches were interested
in having Magic play for their teams.*

Magic continued to flourish on his high school team. He lived up to his nickname with his dazzling play. He not only starred on the team, but he made teammates better as well. He threw pinpoint-accurate passes that converted into easy shots and layups. He shouted words of encouragement. In his sophomore season, Magic led Everett to a 22–2 record. Over the next two seasons, Everett lost only three games total. During Magic's senior season, he led his team to the 1976–77 Michigan Class A State Championship title, while averaging 28.8 points per game. College coaches from across the country came to see him play. He received hundreds of scholarship offers. Now it was decision time. He had to pick the college he would attend.

After weighing his options, Magic limited his choice to two schools: the University of Michigan (known as Michigan) and Michigan State University (known as Michigan State). He wanted to stay close to home, and he was a fan of both schools growing up. As a young teen, he went to Michigan home games on Saturday afternoons to watch the Wolverines and then to Michigan State home games to see the Spartans play at night. He knew whatever school he chose, his family and friends lived close enough to attend his games and cheer him on.

Friends, family, and reporters all **speculated** Magic would choose Michigan. It had the better basketball program of the two schools. Just two seasons earlier, the team had made it to the national championship game of the National Collegiate Athletic Association (NCAA) tournament, before losing to Indiana 86–68.

Michigan State's basketball program was struggling. Its team was coming off a losing season, finishing 12–15, and did not even make it into the NCAA tournament.

Magic called a press conference for April 22, 1977, to announce his college choice. Dozens of reporters were there. "I've decided to attend Michigan . . ."—he took a long pause and continued—"State University."

The reporters were stunned. But Magic later explained his choice: "Michigan thought it had a lot more to offer than Michigan State, which it did. But I like the underdog school. Every team I've played on was not supposed to win. Even when I go to the playground, I don't pick the best players. I pick the players who want to work."

THE SPARK OF THE SPARTANS

When Magic arrived at Michigan State, the Spartans had never won the national title and had not won their conference title outright in 20 years. Magic predicted he would lead his new team to not only the conference title, but the national title as well.

In his freshman year, the Spartans were instantly better. They finished with a 25–5 record and won the championship title of their conference, the Big Ten. (No other Spartan team had ever won more than 20 games in a season.) They lost in the third round of the NCAA tournament to Kentucky—the eventual national champions that season.

Magic's stats were impressive for a freshman. He averaged 17 points, 7.4 assists, and 7.9 rebounds per game and was named to the All-America team. Magic grew as a player and as a person at Michigan State. His coach, Jud Heathcote, was a strict **disciplinarian**. If a player skipped a class or missed a team study hall session, he was benched for the next game. Magic made sure he never missed either.

Heathcote also did not **tolerate** mental mistakes on the court. If Magic messed up a play or missed a defensive assignment, Heathcote yelled "You've got to think!"

The only thing Heathcote liked less than mental mistakes was an excuse. At first, Magic tried to explain to his coach why he made the mistake. But soon Magic learned that when his coach yelled, there was only one correct response: "I blew it Coach, it won't happen again."

Though Magic was tall for the position, he was a natural as a point guard. Heathcote spent hours with his star, working with him on his outside shot, free throws, and passing. In high school, Magic shot a lot when he was off balance. Heathcote helped him put a stop to this bad habit.

"He worked with us individually, and he made us all better players," said Magic about his college coach. "He wanted me running the show, and I was thrilled to do it."

Thanks in part to Heathcote's **mandatory** study halls, Magic excelled in the classroom as well. He majored in telecommunications, with a minor in education. In his first

Magic's skills and energy immediately added a spark to the Spartans' basketball program.

semester, he finished with a 3.4 grade point average (GPA)—a B+ average.

Early in Magic's sophomore season, the Spartans were unstoppable. They won 9 of their first 10 games. But they had a midseason slump in

*In his first year with the Spartans, Magic helped
the team win its conference title.*

January and lost 4 games. They rebounded by the end of the season and
won 10 of their last 11 regular-season games. With Magic leading the way,
Michigan State breezed through the NCAA tournament. The Spartans
found themselves facing Indiana State, an undefeated team that season,

in the national championship game.

Indiana State's star player was a 6-feet-9 (2.1 m) forward named Larry Bird. Bird and Magic were considered the two best players in college basketball. Bird was an ace shooter—he could score from anywhere on the court. Magic and the Spartans were known for their "alley-oop" play. Magic would lob the ball above the basket, and a teammate would jump, grab the ball, and slam it into the hoop.

The buildup to the game was intense. Journalists and fans alike couldn't wait to see these two players face off for the title. More than 35 million

Life & Career Skills

Magic Johnson and Larry Bird have one of the most storied rivalries in sports history. It began during their college days when their teams faced each other in the national championship game in 1979. That same year, both were **drafted** into the NBA. Throughout the 1980s, they were the best NBA players on the best NBA teams.

From 1979 to 1991, Magic and the Los Angeles Lakers faced Bird and the Boston Celtics 37 times. The Lakers won 22 of those games. They played each other 3 times for the NBA Championship: Los Angeles won 2. Bird won 3 NBA MVP awards as did Magic. Despite how intense their competitiveness was (Bird said the first thing he did each morning was check the paper to see how Magic had played the night before), they blossomed into the best of friends.

"Becoming friends with Larry Bird meant a lot to me," Magic once said. "We were still rivals, of course. But there was a warmth that made our competition much more fun." Throughout their careers, they played in charity games together, acted in the same commercials, and sent each other funny notes and gifts.

Every time they played, though, they still wanted to beat each other. But after the game, despite who won or lost, they exchanged handshakes or a hug. "After God and my father," Magic told *Sports Illustrated*, "I respect Larry Bird more than anyone."

people tuned in to their televisions to watch the title game. Everybody wondered which star would lead his team to victory.

The answer became crystal clear immediately after the opening tip. Michigan State's tough defense shut Bird down. He shot just 7 of 21 from the floor. Magic was unstoppable. He finished with 24 points and 7 rebounds while leading his team to a 75–64 victory. After the game, he jumped around and celebrated with his teammates. But while he was celebrating, he glanced over at Bird, who was sitting on the bench with his face in his towel and crying quietly. Magic's heart went out to his rival.

"As happy as I was," said Magic, "I knew that if things had gone just a little differently, I would have been the one sitting there with his face in a towel. I take losses the same way."

Magic turned back to celebrating, but one thought

Magic (left) and his teammate Gregory Kelser celebrate after winning the NCAA championship in March 1979.

lingered in his mind: he was sure he would face Larry Bird again.

STAY OR GO?

Soon after winning the title, Magic faced another decision: should he stay in college or should he turn pro and play in the NBA? His mother wanted him to stay in school and earn his degree. His father wanted him to listen to what the NBA had to offer. Magic felt like he had accomplished everything he could at the college basketball level. He decided to leave college early and go pro.

Magic was drafted as the number one overall pick in the 1979 NBA draft by the Los Angeles Lakers. He received a contract for $500,000 a year. Magic couldn't believe it—he was finally a professional basketball player. He was the happiest he had ever been in his life. Now it was time to prove himself at the highest level of the game. Magic couldn't wait to start playing in the NBA.

Magic always dreamed of playing in the NBA. Despite friends and family telling him how difficult it would be to make it to the NBA, Magic never doubted himself or his ability. He dedicated himself to mastering the sport and reaching his goal. On the first day of the Lakers' training camp, he displayed his strong work ethic by being the first player to arrive at the Forum—the Lakers' home court. He sat in the stands staring down at the hardwood floor, and memory after memory started running through his mind. He recalled playing hoops as a kid and a teenager, then watching NBA games on the couch with his dad. He couldn't believe he was actually an NBA player himself. When the Lakers' trainer Jack Curran escorted Magic to the locker room, Magic spotted his jersey, number 32, for the first time. He tried it on immediately.

"When I looked at myself in the mirror, a member of the Los Angeles Lakers, my eyes filled with tears," Magic said. "That is when it really hit me that I had actually made it."

CHAPTER THREE

SUCCESS ON A NEW COURT

Magic's first couple of months in Los Angeles were some of the toughest in his life. He was used to living in his hometown of Lansing, Michigan, which was small and had only one highway and three main streets. Los Angeles was a gigantic city with more freeways than he could count. He didn't like to go outside for fear he might get lost. Magic also missed his family and friends terribly. This was the first time he had lived so far from home.

Magic (center) is congratulated by his parents after being selected as the number one overall pick in the 1979 NBA draft.

"Sunday nights were the hardest," Magic said. "Even when I was in college, our family always sat down to Sunday dinner together to enjoy fried chicken, black-eyed peas, rice, and apple and sweet-potato pie. Living in California, I missed those dinners more than anything else."

Magic also struggled to adapt his game to the pro level. The competition was a lot more physical than he had ever encountered. Players pushed and shoved hard and no fouls were called. That was just the way the game was played.

Magic's first game as a Laker was a rough one, even before the opening tip-off. During warm-ups, he tripped on his pants and fell flat on his face. His teammates and the crowd laughed loudly at his mishap, and Magic even managed to grin as well.

In the first 17 minutes of play, he made just 1 point. Head coach Jack McKinney took his rookie star out of the game to revive his spirits. When Magic went back in, he found his groove. He finished with 26 points, and Los Angeles beat the San Diego Clippers 103–102 on a last-second shot by Magic's star teammate, center Kareem Abdul-Jabbar.

Magic's play got better and better as the season progressed. His no-look passes became more and more spectacular. His enthusiasm for the game rubbed off on his teammates. Before he joined the team, most of the Lakers were quiet and subdued. Magic, though, was a bundle of energy. He constantly hugged and high-fived teammates, hustled after loose balls, and cheered for everybody. The rookie's passion for the game was **contagious**. Pretty soon, the whole team started to play with Magic's gusto.

Magic was only 20 years old when he played in his first NBA game.

Magic's favorite regular-season game that first year was when the Lakers traveled to Michigan to play the Detroit Pistons. The Lakers won the game easily in front of Magic's family and friends. Best of all, Magic's mom cooked her son's team a dinner of chicken, corn bread, macaroni salad, collard greens, and sweet-potato pie, which was waiting in the locker room after the game ended.

Magic finished the regular season averaging 18 points, 7.3 assists, and 7.7 rebounds per game. He was the first rookie to start in an All-Star game in 11 years. The Lakers won an impressive 60 games during the regular season and cruised through the play-offs, beating the Phoenix Suns and the Seattle SuperSonics. Once again, Magic found himself playing in a championship series, this time in the NBA against the Philadelphia 76ers.

The Lakers led Philadelphia in the series 3–2, when center Abdul-Jabbar was forced to miss Game 6 with a badly sprained ankle. Magic stepped in and took charge, playing center instead of point guard. He scored 42 points, grabbed 15 rebounds, and made 7 assists. He even went 14 of 14 from the free-throw line. The Lakers beat the 76ers 123–107. Magic was the first rookie ever to be named Finals MVP.

"If my first few minutes as a Laker were a total disaster," Magic wrote in his autobiography, *My Life,* "the last game of my rookie year more than made up for it. In fact, the final play-off game against Philadelphia was probably the best performance of my life."

At age 20, Magic Johnson had already won championship titles on the high school, college, and pro level.

SOPHOMORE SETBACK

Magic's second NBA season jumped off to another promising start. In the first month of play, he averaged 21.4 points per game, led the league in steals and assists, and out-rebounded all guards with an average of 8.2 per game. Then in November, Magic suffered the first major setback of his career. During a game against the Atlanta Hawks, a player fell across the back of Magic's left knee, causing it to buckle. Magic needed surgery to repair torn cartilage. He missed close to four months of the season.

For a guy whose life revolved around basketball, this injury was devastating. "It made me see that, just as fast as you can rise to the top, you can come tumbling down," Magic told *Sports Illustrated* after the injury occurred. "First they take your ball away. That's bad. And then, not being around the guys, that really hurts. I mean, you're alone."

Magic had surgery on November 24, 1980, and missed the next 45 games of the season. The Lakers stayed focused without him, going 28–17 in his absence.

Even before his cast was removed, Magic was already preparing for his comeback. He worked his upper body with weights, and as soon as he could put pressure on his knee, he was back in the gym. His first game back was in early March against the New Jersey Nets. When Magic walked on the court, 17,505 Laker fans wearing buttons reading "The Magic is Back" stood up and roared for 45 seconds—1 second for every game their star point guard missed. Magic broke out into one of his biggest smiles ever. He *really* was back!

Although the Lakers beat the Nets that night, Magic didn't have a great game. He made 4 of 12 shots from the field. Even so, his knee looked strong. At first, he was careful and ran **gingerly** up and down the court. But by the end of the game, he was back to his old self—diving for loose balls and leaping for rebounds.

The Lakers finished the season with a 54–28 record but lost in the first round of play-offs to the Houston Rockets. Magic and his teammates were disappointed; they had hoped to defend their crown. Now their sights were set on next season.

Thousands of fans came out to congratulate Magic and his teammates after they won the NBA championship in 1980.

IT'S SHOWTIME!

In November 1981, Magic signed a $25 million, 25-year contract with Los Angeles. He was going to be a Laker for life!

"Obviously the deal would extend well beyond my playing days," said Magic. "[Lakers' owner] Jerry Buss explained that he wanted me to have

Magic (with ball) is famous for his no-look passes.

a good income even after I retired. He also wanted to guarantee me a job with the Lakers."

With his amazing smile and slick skills, Magic led an offense that came to be known as Showtime. It was fast paced and included lots of scoring, lots of fast breaks, and plenty of fun. This style of play also stood out because of its unselfishness. Everybody worked together and won, or lost, as a team. It was easy for the Lakers to play this way because they were such a close-knit team. "We genuinely liked each other, and it showed," said Magic. "Whenever we had a team function, everybody showed. We knew all of this togetherness was a little unusual because guys who were traded to us all said that no team they had been on had as much unity as the Lakers."

Magic's style of play was an example of cooperation. His passing ability was almost an art form. He played like he had eyes all over his head. He rarely looked at the person to whom he was passing; instead, he looked in the opposite direction. He knew where his teammate was heading, and hit him with the pass at just the right second. "There have been times when Magic has thrown passes and I wasn't sure where he was going," said Michael Cooper, Magic's teammate from 1979 to 1990. "Then one of our guys catches the ball and scores, and I run back up the floor convinced that he must've thrown it through somebody." Magic led the league in assists in four different seasons.

At the end of the 1981–82 season, Magic led his team to their second title. They defeated the

Though Magic was an outstanding individual player, he tried to turn the spotlight away from himself and toward other players who also deserved credit. Magic thought of every team he played on as a family. He encouraged his teammates to think the same way.

When Magic was a Laker, the team went out together after games, and there was always nonstop chatter on the bus and plane rides. "It got to the point where if you were going to pick up a sandwich," Magic said, "you practically had to ask 11 other guys what they wanted for lunch."

Magic speculated that the reason his team got along well was because they were winning. But he soon realized that "maybe, it was the other way around."

Philadelphia 76ers again 4–2, just as they did in Magic's rookie year. Magic was named the Finals MVP for a second time. The Lakers made it back to the Finals in 1983 and 1984 but lost both times, once to Philadelphia and once to the Boston Celtics.

Magic wasn't the type of player to get discouraged by losing back-to-back championships. In fact, the losses **motivated** him to become an even better player and teammate. As a result, the four seasons from 1984 through 1988 were the best of his professional career. The Lakers won three NBA titles during this time.

The most magical of these seasons was 1986–87. This was partly because Magic had become the leader of the squad. Previously, center Kareem Abdul-Jabbar was the true head of the team. Abdul-Jabbar had been with the Lakers since 1975 and was one of the sport's best players. But in the fall of 1986, Abdul-Jabbar was 39 years old, and he planned to retire after the 1988–89 season. He wanted Magic to lead the team even before then. During practices that season, Jabbar taught Magic his famous shot—known as the junior hook shot—which Magic soon mastered. With his new shot, which Magic called "junior, junior, hook shot," and the guidance of Abdul-Jabbar, Magic embraced his new leadership role and had the best season of his NBA career.

At the end of the 1986–87 regular season, Magic won his first NBA MVP award after leading the league in assists per game while also scoring 23.9 points per game. He was only the third NBA guard to ever win this award.

"As a team player, I had accomplished everything I wanted to accomplish, but as an individual, something was still missing," Magic said

Magic (number 32) and Larry Bird were fierce competitors on the court.

after he won the award, highlighting its significance to him. It was also especially important to him, because his rival, guard Larry Bird of the Boston Celtics, had already won the award three times. Bird and Magic were the two best players in the league. Magic desperately wanted to win at least one of these awards over Bird. At a news conference, Magic joked, "I'd like to thank Larry for having a slightly off year."

That season, Magic led his team to the NBA Finals against the Boston Celtics. The Lakers won in 6 games, 4–2, and Magic won his third Finals MVP award. (In Game 4 of the 1987 Finals, Magic even used his junior, junior, hook on a last-second shot to win the game for the Lakers.) While the team celebrated, Lakers head coach Pat Riley made a bold statement. He said the Lakers would repeat as champions the following season. Reporters and opposing teams **scoffed** at this remark. Riley made these remarks to motivate his team and try to get them focused on winning again.

The strategy paid off. The Lakers defeated the Detroit Pistons, 4–3, in the 1988 NBA Finals. It was the first time a team won back-to-back titles since the late 1960s. "Riley's plan worked," Magic said. "All season long we kept our eye on that prize, and in the end we were able to get it." After the game, Riley hugged Magic and thanked him for his help. He knew he could not have upheld his guarantee of victory without his star point guard.

Over the next three seasons, the Lakers were still **dominant**. They won at least 50 games during each of these seasons, but they didn't win an NBA championship. Magic still won back-to-back MVP trophies for the 1988–89 and 1989–90 seasons. And, at age 31, he planned to play a couple more seasons, though he was starting to think about his life after basketball. He hoped to become a full-time businessman someday.

Magic started the 1990–91 season with the Lakers. But on November 7, 1991, he shocked the world with a stunning announcement: he had tested positive for **HIV**, the virus that causes **AIDS**. The physical and emotional **rigors** of the NBA season would be too much for his body. He had to retire.

"I spoke from the heart," Magic said to *Sports Illustrated* about his announcement. "I said that because I had tested HIV-positive, I was retiring from the NBA. I also said I was going to beat [AIDS]. And I will."

Fans, friends, and family tried not to doubt Magic's words. If anybody could beat this disease, it was Magic.

The Lakers won back-to-back championships in 1987 and 1988.

Magic has spent his life setting high standards for himself and his teammates. His leadership has helped the teams he has played on to be highly successful. A numerical breakdown of his accomplishments during his 13-season career is impressive. More importantly, it exemplifies his talent, dedication, and ability to work well with others and under pressure.

1   Olympic gold medals won
2   All-Star MVP awards
3   NBA MVP awards
5   NBA championship titles
12 All-Star appearances

CHAPTER FOUR

OFF THE COURT
AND IN THE COMMUNITY

*Through his own organization and others, Magic
promotes HIV awareness and education.*

Magic did not spend any time feeling sorry for himself. He faced his
HIV status with the same courage he displayed playing basketball.

The first thing he did was encourage his wife of two months, Earleatha
"Cookie" Kelly, to get tested. She was seven weeks pregnant. Luckily, she

was not infected, so the baby would not be infected either. Next, Magic read everything he could about the virus and the disease. He wanted to understand what he was up against. In addition, he wanted to help educate the public to prevent others from becoming infected.

"It's my job to help us all understand that the disease is bigger than we think," Magic said to *Sports Illustrated* after his announcement. "I hope that because of my experience people will now learn everything they need to know about the virus. I know that I'm prepared for this new role, because I've always been a teacher in basketball."

Magic joined the National Commission on AIDS run by the White House. He became a national spokesperson in the fight against the disease and made speeches to live audiences and on television. In the spring of 1992, he appeared on a half-hour TV show on Nickelodeon called "A Conversation with Magic Johnson." On the show, he sat down with kids between the ages of 8 and 14 and talked

Life & Career Skills

Magic started the Magic Johnson Foundation in December 1991. The nonprofit charity donates funds to organizations that promote HIV/AIDS education and provide health care. Magic's commitment to the cause was applauded around the world. Through the foundation, he organized a worldwide basketball touring company that also helped raise money and AIDS awareness.

"He's a hero because he didn't just make the announcement and then go away," said Phill Wilson, AIDS coordinator for the city of Los Angeles, in February 1992.

Magic's career with the Lakers—as a player, coach, and part owner—has spanned more than 25 years.

about ways to avoid contracting HIV. He also wrote a book for kids titled *What You Can Do to Avoid AIDS.*

When Magic announced he had HIV, many feared it was a death sentence. But doctors said he could ward off contracting AIDS with the right medical treatment, exercise, and a proper diet. Magic took the medications the doctors prescribed and maintained a strict fitness regimen that included daily full-court basketball games. He also stopped eating red meat and fried foods, and instead loaded up on fruits and vegetables and grilled or broiled chicken.

In February 1992, four months after announcing his retirement, he showed no signs of weakness or fatigue, which are symptoms of AIDS. In fact, he felt so healthy that he decided to play in the 1992 NBA All-Star Game. And he played marvelously, scoring 25 points and making 9 assists. He was named the game's MVP as his team—which represented the Western Conference of the NBA—defeated the stars of the Eastern Conference 153–113. The game was

21st Century Content

Before Magic learned he was HIV-positive, he had committed to play for the U.S. men's basketball team at the 1992 Summer Olympics in Barcelona, Spain. This was the first Olympics in which professional basketball players from the United States were allowed to compete. Feeling healthy, Magic decided to uphold his commitment and play. The U.S. squad, dubbed the Dream Team, was considered the greatest team ever assembled. They cruised through the tournament, beating opponents by an average of 44 points per game. They went 8–0 and easily won the gold medal.

Magic and his teammates, including Larry Bird and Michael Jordan, were as popular as rock stars at the Games. Opponents snapped photos of the U.S. team before games even started. Everywhere Magic went, he heard the same request: "Ma-jeek! Ma-jeek! Please smile for me. Smile for the camera." Magic said, "I'll hear that in my sleep."

Magic was honored that people from around the world knew and liked him. He also felt extremely lucky that he was healthy enough to be a part of the Olympic experience. "I [was thankful for] the strength and the opportunity to come back, to play basketball again, and to be part of the whole magnificent Olympic experience," Magic said. "It's a memory I will always cherish."

*As part of the Dream Team, Magic won a gold
medal at the 1992 Summer Olympics.*

"a moment to cherish," pointed out Clyde Drexler, Magic's All-Star
teammate. Magic played again in the summer of 1992 for the U.S. Men's
Olympic basketball team. The team took home the gold.

MAGIC'S BUSINESS VENTURES

After the Olympics, Magic didn't play much competitive basketball for the next four years. He did not stay out of the game completely though. In 1994, he returned to the NBA briefly as a coach for the Lakers during their last 16 regular-season games. The team went 5–11 under his guidance. After the season ended, Magic decided coaching was not for him.

Magic had plenty of other ways to stay busy. He spent time with his sons, Andre, born February 20, 1981, and Earvin III, born June 4, 1992. He and Cookie also adopted a daughter, Elisa, in January 1995.

Outside of his work with his foundation, Magic threw himself into other positive business projects such as ones that helped renew communities. His company, Magic Johnson Enterprises, which he started in 1992, focuses on urban business development and oversees several other businesses and partnerships that he has formed. In 1994, he opened the Magic Johnson Movie Theaters in the African American community of Crenshaw in Los Angeles, where many big movie chains wouldn't open theaters. They believed that only theaters in more **affluent**, white communities would make money. Magic thought differently. The theater sparked a revival in the tough Los Angeles neighborhood. Following Magic's lead, more businesses opened around the theater. By February 1996, Magic's movie complex was one of the top five in the country in gross revenues.

Magic believes that you can make money while improving communities—and he didn't stop at just one movie theater. One of his corporations, Johnson Development Corporation, has joined with large restaurant chains, including Starbucks and T.G.I. Friday's, to bring stores to 65 lower-income areas around the country. The businesses have been smashing successes and, like his first movie theater, have helped to revive downtrodden areas.

"A lot of athletes open one restaurant with their name on it," says Jerry Buss, the owner of the Lakers. "Compare that to having an empire [like Magic does]."

RETURN TO THE COURT

Though Magic enjoys his business ventures, his first love will always be basketball. In January 1996, he returned to the NBA as a player because he missed the game so much. When he retired because of his HIV status, people told him that playing basketball would kill him. "Well," Magic said, "not playing basketball was killing me."

His first game back was on January 30. He was 4 years older and 30 pounds (13.6 kilograms) heavier than when he last played professionally, but he competed with his usual flair. He scored 19 points and dished out 10 assists. Magic played 32 games with the Lakers that season and averaged 6.9 assists and 14.6 points per game. After the Houston Rockets ousted Los Angeles in the first round of the playoffs, he retired from basketball for good. In 2002, within 7 years of his last professional game, Magic was inducted into the Basketball Hall of Fame.

Today, Magic is vice president and part owner of the Lakers. He feels like the Los Angeles club, as well as the entire NBA, is his extended family. "When you face a crisis you know who your true friends are," Magic said.

The support of Magic's family has been central to his success.

His former teammates, coaches, and opponents have supported him throughout his career as well as in his battle with HIV. He hopes he'll always be there for them as well.

CHAPTER FIVE

FUTURE AND LEGACY

Magic was honored with a star on the Hollywood Walk of Fame for having started a chain of movie theaters across the United States.

One of the most successful players in basketball history, Magic Johnson is also one of the most successful businessmen in the world. His net worth is estimated at $800 million.

Magic continues to bring new businesses to urban areas. In August 2006, he opened up a fitness club **franchise** in a downtrodden part of Oakland, California. More than 1,000 club members attended the opening. A Starbucks store, which is one of the many operated jointly by Johnson Development Corporation and Starbucks, opened in the same neighborhood. The coffee hot spot is one of the highest-grossing stores in the entire

Learning & Innovation Skills

Many of Magic's business projects include collaborations with other companies and often require him to speak before diverse groups of people, like community leaders and investors. His ability to effectively articulate his ideas has contributed to his business success.

Magic joined talk show host Larry King on a special to discuss aid to victims of Hurricane Katrina. The Magic Johnson Foundation contributed to relief efforts.

Magic is enthusiastic about each of his many business ventures.

Starbucks chain. "I don't really listen to what people say about urban America," Magic said at the opening of his new gym. "I know they're wrong."

Magic's charity work also continues to thrive. Through the Magic Johnson Foundation, in addition to raising money for AIDS awareness and research, he provides funding to send underprivileged minorities to college. As of August 2006, the foundation had provided scholarships to 225 young people in colleges around the nation.

On December 1, 2006, Magic launched a $60 million partnership with Abbott Laboratories, a drug company. The partnership, announced on World AIDS Day, aims to cut the number of new HIV infections among African Americans by 50 percent in the next five years. They hope to do so through educational programs as well as by providing scholarships to doctors to staff HIV/AIDS clinics in African American communities.

In addition to his urban development businesses and his charity work, Magic has his own clothing and sneaker line called Magic32. He started the company because he thought there was a "void in the marketplace for a high-quality shoe at an affordable price." Magic's basketball sneakers sell for about $50, as opposed to $100 or $150 for those sold by Nike and Adidas.

Life & Career Skills

Magic embraces new adventures and business undertakings. Most times, these are successful. But he failed miserably when he tried something new in 1998. He hosted his own television talk show, *The Magic Hour*.

The show debuted on June 8, 1998, and critics and fans alike disapproved immediately. Critics said Magic's lack of television experience showed—he looked uncomfortable interviewing guests and had trouble keeping the conversation flowing smoothly. The show seemed boring and lifeless. As a result, its ratings were low, and it was cancelled after just eight weeks. Magic was embarrassed, but he never regretted doing the show. "The TV show wasn't successful," he said. "But so what? I'm the one who will take chances, not worry about the backlash. The day after the show ended, it was on to something else."

Taking on new challenges is what's important to him. In the end, failing or succeeding didn't matter.

Magic and his wife, Cookie, met while in college at Michigan State. They've been married for more than 15 years.

People continue to marvel at Magic's post-playing success. He simply credits his achievements to his basketball career being cut short and his desire to be a positive influence in society. "I got turned on when people said, 'It's all over for Magic,'" he explained. "I wanted to show them I wasn't going away."

More than 15 years after his **diagnosis**, Magic has defied the odds and is as strong as ever. He works out regularly, eats a healthy diet, and continues to take medication. He will always remain HIV-positive, but he has never shown any symptoms of AIDS, such as weight loss, skin blotches, or low energy.

In his future, he sees a long life surrounded by loving family and filled with more business and charity ventures. "It's really wonderful how my life has evolved," Magic once told *Sports Illustrated*. "I wouldn't change anything."

21st Century Content

Magic is known for his attention to detail in his business dealings—every day, he likes to know how much popcorn sells at his movie theaters. He checks each and every outgoing expense closely. Other people might find his actions **tedious**, but Magic explains his intense observation this way: "It's my name and my money," he says. "I don't mess around with that."

TIMELINE

1959 Earvin Johnson Jr. is born in Lansing, Michigan, on August 14.

1977 Magic leads Everett High School to the Michigan Class A State Championship title. He announces he will attend Michigan State University.

1979 Magic leads Michigan State to victory over Indiana State 75–64 for the NCAA title. He is chosen as the number one overall pick in the NBA draft.

1980 The Lakers win the NBA championship (it is Magic's first with the team). He is named the Finals MVP. The following season, he has surgery on his knee and misses the next 45 games.

1981 Magic's son Andre is born on February 20.

1982 The Lakers win the NBA championship. Magic wins the Finals MVP award.

1985 The Lakers win the NBA championship.

1987 The Lakers win the NBA championship. Magic wins his first NBA MVP award and is named the Finals MVP.

1988 The Lakers win the NBA championship.

1989 Magic wins the NBA MVP award.

1990 Magic wins the NBA MVP award.

1991 Magic marries his longtime girlfriend, Earleatha "Cookie" Kelly, on September 14. On November 7, he announces he is HIV-positive and retires from the NBA. He founds the Magic Johnson Foundation.

1992 Magic and Cookie's son Earvin III is born on June 4. Magic and the Dream Team win the gold medal at the Summer Olympics in Barcelona, Spain. Magic forms Johnson Development Corporation.

1994 Magic becomes part owner and a vice president of the Lakers.

1995 Magic and Cookie adopt a daughter, Elisa, in January.

1996 Magic returns to the NBA to play for the Lakers for 32 games.

2002 Magic Johnson is inducted into the Naismith Basketball Hall of Fame on September 28.

2006 On December 1, Magic launches a $60 million partnership with a drug company that aims to cut the number of new HIV infections among African Americans by 50 percent in the next 5 years.

Glossary

affluent (AF-loo-uhnt) having an abundance of wealth, property, or other material goods

AIDS (adz) acquired immunodeficiency syndrome; a disease of the immune system

contagious (kuhn-TAY-juhss) quickly passed from person to person; could be something like laughter, joy, or illness

diagnosis (dye-uhg-NOH-sis) the process of determining by examination the nature of a disease or condition

disciplinarian (dis-uh-pluh-NAIR-ee-uhn) a person who enforces rules and codes of conduct

dominant (DOM-uh-nuhnt) being in a commanding or elevated position

drafted (DRAF-ted) selected by a system in which rights to new players are divided and shared among professional teams

franchise (FRAN-cheyez) the rights or licenses granted by a company to an individual or group to market its products or services in a specific territory

gingerly (JIN-jer-lee) doing something with great care or caution; carefully

HIV (ACH-EYE-VEE) human immunodeficiency virus; the virus that causes AIDS

mandatory (MAN-duh-tawr-ee) required as a matter of duty or responsibility

motivated (MO-tuh-vay-ted) to cause someone to act in a positive way for a reason or set goal; to provide with a motive

rigors (RIG-erz) hardships due to a certain way of life or living condition

scoffed (SKOFD) to not take an idea or statement seriously; to laugh or make fun of something

speculated (SPEK-yuh-lay-ted) pondered or guessed

tedious (TEE-dee-us) long and boring

tolerate (TOHL-uh-rayt) to allow the existence or practice

FOR MORE INFORMATION

Books

Gottfried, Ted. *Earvin Magic Johnson: Champion and Crusader*. New York: Franklin Watts, 2001.

Haskins, James. *Sports Great: Magic Johnson*. Rev. and exp. ed. Hillside, NJ: Enslow Publishers, 1992.

Johnson, Earvin. *My Life: Earvin "Magic" Johnson with William Novak*. New York: Random House, 1992.

Web Sites

Basketball Hall of Fame
www.hoophall.com
For biographies of members of the Hall of Fame, including players, coaches, and more

Magic Johnson Foundation
www.magicjohnson.org
Features information about the foundation's mission and programs as well as many images of Magic

NBA Encyclopedia, Playoff Edition
www.nba.com/history/players/magic_johnson_nba50_pt1.html
Includes an interview with Magic

INDEX

ABOUT THE AUTHOR

Ellen Labrecque is a freelance writer living outside of New York City. She has written other books including *World's Greatest Athletes: Surfing* and *World's Greatest Athletes: Ice Hockey*. Previously, she was a senior editor at *Sports Illustrated For Kids* magazine for eight years.